IS IT SAFE TO DRINK THE WATER?

A GUIDE TO SANTA FE

IS IT SAFE TO DRINK THE WATER?

A GUIDE TO SANTA FE

MARCIA MUTH

SECOND EDITION, Revised & Enlarged
Printed in the United States of America

Library of Congress Cataloging in Publication Data:

Muth, Marcia (1919-).
Is it safe to drink the water?

Recommended Reading: pp. 24-25.
1. Santa Fe (N.M.)—Description—Guide-books. 2. Santa Fe (N.M.)—History. I. Title.
F804.S23M87 1983 917.89'56 83-9212
ISBN 0-86534-025-0

Published in 1983 by Sunstone Press / Post Office Box 23321 / Santa Fe, New Mexico 87504-2321

TABLE OF CONTENTS

Dedicated to Steve and George
who share my love of Santa Fe

HISTORY

When was Santa Fe founded?

In 1610 by Don Pedro de Peralta.

Were there people living here before 1610?

Yes, there were Indians here in prehistoric times, and Spanish colonists came up from Mexico as early as 1598.

How long has Santa Fe been a capital city?

Since 1610 Santa Fe has served as the center for Spanish, Indian, Mexican and American governments. For a brief period (two weeks) the capital was occupied by Confederate forces.

Were the Spanish able to stay in New Mexico?

No, in 1680 there was an Indian revolt. The Spanish were driven out.

When did the Spanish return and who led them?

They returned in 1692, led by Don Diego De Vargas.

What does Santa Fe mean?

"Holy faith." Tradition says that the name has been shortened from "La Villa Real de la Santa Fe de San Francisco" (The Royal City of the Holy Faith of St. Francis)

When did Santa Fe come under Mexican rule?

In 1821 when Mexico won her independence from Spain, New Mexico became a Mexican province.

When was Santa Fe conquered for the United States and by whom?

On August 18, 1846 General Stephen W. Kearny marched his American troops into Santa Fe and took over the city. The war between Mexico and the United States had begun in April 1846.

When did Santa Fe become the territorial capital?

1851. New Mexico was created a territory by the U.S. Congress on Sept. 9, 1850 and on March 3, 1851, the Territorial government was organized.

When was Santa Fe incorporated as a city?

July 4, 1851.

Were there any Civil War battles fought here?

Not in Santa Fe but near by there was a battle at Glorieta Pass on March 8, 1862. The Confederate Army was defeated in Apache Canyon (about 15 miles from Santa Fe) and Santa Fe recaptured for the Union.

When did New Mexico become a state?

January 6, 1912; 47th state to join the Union.

When did the Santa Fe Trail start and did it come into town?

It started in 1822 and the end of the trail was at the Plaza.

Where did the Santa Fe Trail start?

In Franklin, Missouri, near St. Louis.

When did the railroad come to Santa Fe?

On February 9, 1880 an 18-mile spur was extended from Lamy to Santa Fe by the Atchison, Topeka and Santa Fe Railroad. In 1885, the main line of the Denver, and Rio Grande Western Railroad was extended to Santa Fe.

SANTA FE TODAY

What is the population of Santa Fe?

48,953 (1980 census, and still growing!)

What is the altitude?

6,990 feet (higher in some parts of the city)

What is the weather like in the summer?

Average temperature ranges from 52 to 80 degrees. It is warm (sometimes hot) in the day but cool in the morning and at night. It rains during July, August, and September in the afternoon, but usually the rain does not last for more than a short time. Cloudy days are a rarity!

What is the weather like in the winter?

Average temperature ranges from 19 to 50 degrees. The snowfall is principally in the mountains but there is also snow in town and it may stay on the ground for several days. Winters seem less severe because of the predominantly sunny days and low humidity.

What kind of city government does Santa Fe have?

City manager, mayor, and council.

What are the main sources of income and employment in Santa Fe?

State government, tourism, education. Secondary sources are construction, arts and crafts, and food service.

Are there any colleges in Santa Fe?

Yes, two. The College of Santa Fe, a four-year liberal arts, co-educational college operated by the Christian Brothers, founded as St. Michael's College in 1859. St. John's College of Santa Fe, four-year liberal arts, non-denominational western branch of St. John's College in Annapolis, Maryland. St. John's was founded in Maryland in 1696 and opened its Santa Fe doors in 1964.

What other educational institutions are located in Santa Fe?

In addition to the public and Catholic school systems, there are the New Mexico School for the Deaf, the Institute of American Indian Arts, St. Catherine Indian School, All Indian Pueblo Council Santa Fe Indian School, Santa Fe Preparatory School, Rio Grande School, the Brunn School, New School of Santa Fe. Southwestern College of Life Sciences, Santa Fe School of Music, and several other private grade and specialized schools for children and adults.

What is Santa Fe's nickname?

The City Different.

Where is the Chamber of Commerce located?

200 W. Marcy St.

Where can I get city maps?

At the Chamber of Commerce, bookstores, hotel newsstands and some stores. The Palace of the Governors gives out a map of the downtown area.

Where can I get topographic maps?

At surplus and sports stores.

How many museums are there in Santa Fe?

Five. The Palace of the Governors (Plaza) has historical and archaeological exhibits. The Museum of Fine Arts (Plaza) has a permanent collection of New Mexico art plus changing loan exhibits. The Museum of International Folk Art (Camino Lejo) has exhibits relating to folk art of the world plus a new wing housing objects from the Girard Collection of Folk Art. The Wheelwright Museum of the American Indian (Camino Lejo) has exhibits of Indian art. The Institute of American Indian Arts (Cerrillos Rd.) has exhibits of contemporary Indian art. (The Laboratory of Anthropology is next to the Museum of International Folk Art and while not a museum in the traditional sense, has exhibits of pottery, silver, textiles, and baskets.)

Is there a zoo in Santa Fe?

No.

SPECIAL EVENTS, FESTIVALS, ETC.

NOTE: Dates vary each year for most these events; check with the Chamber of Commerce for the exact dates.

What and when is the Fiesta de Santa Fe?

The Fiesta celebrates the 1692 reconquest of New Mexico by de Vargas. It is the oldest community celebration in the United States, having started in 1712. It combines religious and secular elements. There are religious processions and masses; a Fiesta queen and her court; parades; dancing; mariachi music; a melodrama; food booths; arts and crafts displays; and a reenactment of de Vargas' entry into Santa Fe. It is held on a weekend in September.

Who is Zozobra?

Zozobra or "Old Man Gloom" is a huge (over 40 feet tall) figure made of lumber, chicken wire, paper, and muslin. The burning of this figure signals the start of Fiesta. His burning is accompanied by spectacular fireworks. The custom started in 1926 and was originated by Will Shuster. The Kiwanis Club now sponsors this part of Fiesta.

When is the Indian Market?

See information in section on INDIANS.

When is the Rodeo de Santa Fe?

The Rodeo de Santa Fe is held every year in July. It lasts for four days. A parade is held the first day in the downtown area. Other Rodeo events include the crowning of the Rodeo queen, dances, and all the usual rodeo events. Rodeo grounds are at the south end of town on Rodeo road.

What is displayed at the Spanish Market?

The Spanish Market emphasizes traditional Spanish colonial crafts. Among the crafts will be stitchery, iron work, tin craft, weaving, and woodcarving. The market is held annually in July under the Portal of the Palace of the Governors.

Does Santa Fe have some unique Christmas customs?

Yes. Homes, businesses, and public buildings are decorated with farolitos (far-o-lee-toes) which are brown paper sacks filled with sand and containing a burning candle. Today many large buildings use electric farolitos, sacks containing small light bulbs. Farolitos are placed on walls, rooftops, and along walks and driveways. Small bonfires called luminarias are also seen along walks and roads. They are made of criss-crossed sticks of wood and are from two to three feet high. There are also folk plays (Los Pastores) which act out the Christmas story.

What is the Santa Fe Festival of the Arts?

A city-wide celebration of the arts held in October. It features a large art exhibit held in the Sweeney Convention Center and special exhibits throughout the city in galleries and public buildings. There are also lectures, films, and other related activities.

Where is the Santa Fe Opera?

Five miles to the north of the city. This outdoor theater has opera performances during July and August. Its first season was in 1957. The original building burned in 1967 and during that season all the remaining performances were held in Sweeney Gymnasium. The new opera building was completed in time for the 1968 season. Outstanding professional singers from all over the world make up the roster of the opera casts. The orchestra, stage designers and directors are also well-known professionals.

What events are connected with the Chamber Music Festival?

The Santa Fe Chamber Music Festival, started in 1973, features concerts, recitals, lectures and symposiums. Outstanding soloists and composers take part in each summer's programs. Saturday morning rehearsals are free and open to the public.

What is the Santa Fe Festival Theater?

A professional repertory company giving a series of plays during July and August. Plays are given in the Armory For the Arts on Old Pecos Trail.

In addition to the events and festivals listed, there are many other groups that sponsor musical, dramatic, and artistic programs . . . . . the Orchestra of Santa Fe; Santa Fe Desert Chorale; the Dallas Ballet; British American Theatre Institute; the Santa Fe Film Festival; the Santa Fe Childrens' Project; Theatre Intime; and Black Mesa Ensemble; are just a few examples of the cultural fare available to residents and visitors. The Santa Fe Community Theatre and the Santa Fe Community Orchestra also give a series of public performances.

FOOD

What is the origin of the type of "native" food served here?

Spanish, Mexican and Indian cookery have all influenced New Mexico dishes resulting in a unique and distinctive cuisine that is primarily based on the chili pepper.

What is salsa?

Red or green chili sauce.

Which is hotter, red or green chili?

It varies according to the peppers used. If you ask your waiter or waitress, they will tell you which is hotter at that particular time.

What are the flat, round "pancakes" served as bread or in dishes?

Tortillas (tor-tee-yahs). These are made from flour or cornmeal. A side dish of flour tortillas is served instead of bread or toast. Flour tortillas rolled and filled with meat and/or beans are called burritos. They are covered with red or green chili. Corn tortillas are used in tacos, enchilidas, and chalupas. They are covered or filled with beef or chicken, beans, lettuce and cheese. Don't be alarmed if your tortillas are blue—they are made from blue cornmeal. Also in this area, enchiladas are often served flat rather than rolled.

What are tostados (tohs-tah-dos)?

Little, crisp corn tortillas served with salsa as an appetizer. They are also used in some dishes and usually served with guacamole.

What are sopaipillas (so-pah-pee-yahs)?

A deep-fried bread that forms into a hollow "pillow" as it puffs up when fried. You bite off one end and pour honey into it. They are also served stuffed with meat, beans and chili.

What are frijoles (free-ho-leez)?

Beans, usually pinto beans. Frijoles refritos are refried beans.

What does the phrase "con queso" (con kay-so) mean?

With cheese.

What does the phrase "con arroz" (ah-rros) mean?

With rice.

What is arroz con Pollo (ah-rros kon poy-yoh)?

Chicken with rice.

What is carne adovada?

A pork dish with chili.

What are huevos (whey-vos)?

Eggs.

What are huevos rancheros?

Fried eggs with chili.

What is guacamole (wha-ka-mo-lee)?

An avocado dish served as a salad or dip.

What is menudo (may-new-dough)?

Tripe in a stew or soup dish.

What is posole (po-so-lee)?

Hominy with pork and chili.

What are chili rellenos (ray-e-nos)?

Green chiles filled with cheese, dipped in batter and fried.

What are tamales (tah-mahl-lehs)?

Pork and red chili in a layer of cornmeal mush, usually placed in a cornhusk and cooked in a red chili sauce.

What are tacos (tah-kohs)?

Fried, crisp tortillas folded and filled with beef or chicken, beans, lettuce, chopped tomatoes and grated cheese.

What is chorizo (choh-ree-soh)?

Seasoned pork sausage.

What are jalapenos (hal-lah-peh-nyos)?

Small, green very hot peppers.

What are nachos?

Corn chips topped with cheese and sometimes jalapenos and served as an appetizer.

What is flan?

A custard covered with carmel sauce.

What are biscochitos (bisk-ko-chee-toes)?

Anise seed cookies.

What are empanadas (ehm-pah-nah-dahs)?

Small pastries filled with meat or fruit.

What is sopa?

Bread pudding with cinnamon and raisins.

What is mole (moh-leh)?

Mexican chocolate sauce.

Are pinon nuts good to eat?

Yes. They can also be used in cooking and are specially good in fudge. They may be eaten raw or roasted. Although they are always available, there is a bumper crop every seven years in Santa Fe.

DINING OUT

Are there many places to dine out in Santa Fe?

Yes. In fact, there are more than we can possibly list. One of the fun things to do in Santa Fe is to try different restaurants and make your own list of favorite places. All we can do is give you some suggestions to start you on your gastronomical tour.

Do I need to make reservations?

Many of the restaurants do require reservations especially during the busy summer tourist season. Since some restaurants serve only lunch, some lunch and dinner only and closed days vary, it is advisable to telephone in advance if you are not sure.

Do all restaurants serve Spanish (New Mexican) food?

No, but many do have some Spanish dishes on their menu while others are noted for their Spanish food.

Where can I get that authentic New Mexican cooking?

La Tertulia (416 Agua Fria)
Tomasita's (500 Guadalupe)
The Pink Adobe (406 Old Santa Fe Trail)
Josie's Casa de Comida (95 W. Marcy)
Tia Sophia's (125 W. San Francisco)
The Shed (113½ E. Palace Ave.)
Maria's Mexican Cooking (555 W. Cordova Rd.)
El Patio Restaurant (125 E. Water)

Where can I find that special "Santa Fe" atmosphere?

The Pink Adobe (406 Old Santa Fe Trail)
The Bull Ring (414 Old Santa Fe Trail)
La Plazuela (La Fonda)
Staab House at La Posada (330 E. Palace Ave.)
Guadalupe Cafe (313 Guadalupe)
Tecolote Cafe (1203 Cerrillos Rd.)

Where can I get Italian food?

Victor's Ristorante Italiano (423 W. San Francisco)
Mama Lola's Italian Restaurant (548 Agua Fria)
Geppetto's (84 E. San Francisco) (On the Plaza)

Are there any Oriental restaurants in Santa Fe?

Shohko Cafe (Japanese) (321 Johnson)
Taro's of Santa Fe (Japanese) (321 W. San Francisco)
The Saigon Cafe (Vietnamese) (418½ Montezuma)
Peking Palace (Chinese) (1710 Cerrillos Rd.)
Bamboo Chopsticks (Chinese) (2841 Cerrillos Rd.)

I like French or continental cooking, where should I go?

The Compound (653 Canyon Rd.)
Chez Edouard (239 Johnson St.)
Palace Restaurant (Burro Alley and Palace Ave.)
Comme Chez Vous (133 W. Water St.)
Le Mirage (669 Canyon Rd.)

Where can I go for a leisurely dinner?

The Compound (653 Canyon Rd.)
Cassidy's (100 Sandoval, in the Hilton)
The Pink Adobe (406 Old Santa Fe Trail)
Ernie's (731 Canyon Rd.)
Staab House at La Posada (330 E. Palace Ave.)

Palace Restaurant (Burro Alley and Palace Ave.)
The Haven (613 Canyon Rd.)
The Steaksmith (210 Don Gaspar)
The Periscope (2211 Shelby) (Sat. only)

Do many places serve seafood?

Most places have one or two seafood dishes on their menu. Two restaurants that specialize in seafood are:

Plaza Ore House (50 Lincoln Ave.) (On the Plaza)
Chez Renee's Captain's Table (3364 Cerrillos Rd.)

I am on a limited budget, where can I get an inexpensive sandwich or meal in the downtown area?

Delores' (213 Washington Ave.)
Woolworth (58 E. San Francisco) (On the Plaza)
Plaza Restaurant (54 Lincoln Ave.) (On the Plaza)
Little Chief Restaurant (227 Don Gaspar) (At El Centro)
El Patio Restaurant (125 E. Water)

Will being a vegetarian cause me any problems when eating out in Santa Fe?

No. Most restaurants have some non-meat dishes that will suit the vegetarian diet or they will have soup and salad bars. Two restaurants that specialize in natural foods are:

La Paloma (225 E. De Vargas)
Natural Cafe (1494 Cerrillos Rd.)

Are there any cafeterias in Santa Fe?

Furr's Cafeteria (DeVargas Mall)
Furr's Cafeteria (Coronada Shopping Center)

Are there any fast food places in Santa Fe?

Almost all the national fast food chains are represented in Santa Fe and they can be found along Cerrillos Road. Note: A New Mexico chain family restaurant, Goody's is at 3011 Cerrillos Rd.

Are there some restaurants just outside Santa Fe, within easy driving distance?

Yes, several.

El Gancho (Old Las Vegas Highway)
Bishop's Lodge (Bishop's Lodge Rd.)
Rancho Encantado (Tesuque)
El Nido (Tesuque)
Las Brazas (Taos Highway, about 10 miles from Santa Fe)
Rancho de Chimayo (Chimayo, 25 miles north of Santa Fe)

Where can I get additional information on Santa Fe restaurants?

More information can be found in the yellow pages of the telephone book; also in copies of **The Santa Fean,** *and in the local newspapers.*

ARCHITECTURE

What are the two traditional styles of architecture found in Santa Fe?

Pueblo and territorial. Pueblo-style houses are "softer" with rounded lines; territorial houses have brick coping. Both types have flat roofs.

What are adobe (uh-dough-bee) bricks make of?

Earth, sand and straw.

Do houses made of adobe last?

Yes, but only in an arid or semi-arid climate such as Santa Fe. The "oldest house" on De Vargas is a prime example.

What are the round beams called?

Vigas (vee-guhs).

What are latias (lah-tee-uhs)?

Small branches or split sticks laid in a pattern on top of vigas to form the ceiling.

What is the little outdoor oven called?

Horno (or-no).

What is the name of the corner adobe fireplace?

Beehive.

What is the name of the rain spout used on Santa Fe houses)?

Canale (ka-nal-ee).

What is the porch called?

Portal (por-tahl).

What is the entryway called?

Zaguan (zuh-gwan).

Are all buildings that look like adobe made out of adobe?

No, some are frame and some are concrete blocks but they are covered with cement and an earth-tone pigment stucco finish to give the appearance of adobe.

Where are some of the best examples of Santa Fe architecture?

Palace of the Governors (1610) - on the Plaza
Sena Plaza (1831) - Palace Avenue
The Oldest House - De Vargas St.

San Miguel Mission (1610) - Old Santa Fe Trail
State Capitol (1966) - Old Santa Fe Trail
La Fonda (1920) - Plaza
Museum of Fine Art (1917, remodeled 1982) - Plaza
Cristo Rey Church (1939) - Canyon Road

Also walking along E. De Vargas, Canyon Road or E. Palace Avenue will give glimpses of many old adobe homes, most of which are still private residences.

CHURCHES

Are all denominations represented in Santa Fe?

Yes, all the major Christian denominations and some minor ones, have churches or meeting places here. In addition, there are interdenominational and nondenominational churches. There are also Buddhist sects that meet regularly.

Is there a Jewish synagogue?

Yes, Temple Beth Shalom on E. Barcelona Rd.

Where can I find out information about religious services?

The telephone book (yellow pages); the local paper **(New Mexican)** *has news of local churches and their services in the Friday edition. Most hotels/motels also have lists of local churches, their addresses and telephone numbers.*

When was the Cathedral of St. Francis built?

The cornerstone was laid in 1869 on the site of an earlier church built in 1622 and destroyed in the Pueblo Revolt in 1680. A second church was built in 1713 and part of it was incorporated into the Cathedral. An addition was added in the late 1960 s. The Cathedral is one block east of the Plaza.

Who directed the building of the Cathedral?

Archbishop John B. Lamy (1814-1888) who was the model for Bishop La Tour in Willa Cather's book, **Death Comes For the Archbishop.** *Archbishop Lamy is buried under the main altar. A statue of him is in front of the Cathedral.*

When was San Miguel Mission built?

San Miguel (Old Santa Fe Trail and De Vargas) was built around 1621. It was partially destroyed in 1680 and later restored. Because of its age, it is known as the "oldest church."

When was Loretto Chapel built?

In 1873. Also known as Our Lady of Light Chapel, it contains the "miraculous staircase", a spiral stairway built without nails or other support by a mysterious stranger who disappeared soon after completing the work. The

Chapel is now part of the Inn of Loretto motel complex located on the Old Santa Fe Trail, one block south of the Plaza.

When was Cristo Rey Church built?

In 1939. It is the largest adobe building in the country (unless one considers the communal dwelling at Taos Pueblo a single building). The walls vary from two to seven feet in thickness. Stone reredos (the bas-relief sculpture behind the altar) were created by Mexican craftsmen and artists in 1761 and were originally part of the Cathedral. Cristo Rey Church is located on Canyon Road.

Who is La Conquistadora?

La Conquistadora (Our Lady of the Conquest) is a religious image first brought to this area in 1625 by Fray Alonso de Benavides. She may be seen at the Cathedral in a special Chapel except for one week in the Spring when, with religious processions, La Conquistadora is taken to the chapel at Rosario Cemetery for a nine-day novena and then back again to the Cathedral.

INDIANS

What kind of Indians live near Santa Fe?

The Pueblo Indians.

What does the word pueblo mean?

It is a Spanish word meaning village or people.

What are the names of the Indian pueblos nearest Santa Fe and where are they located?

Santo Domingo, 32 miles south of Santa Fe; Cochiti (Coach-it-tee) 28 miles south; Tesuque (Tah-su-kee), 10 miles north; San Ildefonso, 22 miles northwest; Nambe (Nahm-bay), 23 miles north; Santa Clara, 27 miles north; San Juan (San Whan), 30 miles north; Pojoaque (Poh-walk-key), 16 miles north but the pueblo is no longer in existence although Indians still live in the area. These are general directions, consult your map for exact directions.

What are the names of the other pueblos in New Mexico and where are they located?

Picuris (Pee-cur-reese), 20 miles south of Taos; Taos (Touse), 2 miles north of the village of Taos; Acoma (Ah-ko-ma), 56 miles west of Albuquerque; Isleta (Ees-leh-ta), 13 miles south of Albuquerque; Jemez (Haymess), 20 miles northwest of Bernalillo; Laguna, 40 miles west of Albuquerque; Sandia, 14 miles north of Albuquerque; San Felipe, 30 miles north of Albuquerque; Santa Ana, 8 miles northwest of Bernalillo; Zia (Zee-ah), 16 miles northwest of Bernalillo; Zuni, 40 miles south of Gallup.

What are the Pueblo languages?

Tewa (Tay-wa) in San Ildefonso, Santa Clara, San Juan, Nambe, Tesuque, and

Pojoaque. Tiwa (Tee-wa) in Picuris, Taos, Isleta, and Sandia. Keres (Kay-rays) in Cohiti, Santo Domingo, Acoma, Laguna, San Felipe, Santa Ana, and Zia. Towa in Jemez and Zunian (Zoon-ye-un) in Zuni.

Can "outsiders" visit the pueblos?

Yes, although you must go to the Governor's office to get a permit and to find out about local restrictions. Santo Domingo prohibits photographs being taken; other pueblos charge a fee. Permission must also be sought and permits purchased for sketching, recording equipment, etc. The Santa Fe Chamber of Commerce has information on the dates of ceremonial dances which are open to the public.

Who governs the pueblo?

The chief civil authority is the governor assisted by a lieutenant-governor in some pueblos, and by a council. The officers and council members are elected officials. Women can be and have been elected as governors.

Where do the Indians live who sit under the portal of the Palace of the Governors?

Most of them come from the nearby pueblos.

How long have the pueblos been here?

Probably since 950 A.D. or before. Present-day pueblos have been occupied since about the 14th century.

What is a kachina (ka-chee-na)?

Kachinas are supernatural beings, some 300 major spirits in Indian (Hopi) religion. They are represented in rituals by costumed dancers. They are also dolls used to teach Indian children the legends. Kachina dolls are also carved and sold to tourists and collectors.

What is a kiva (key-vah)?

A circular underground chamber which is used for ceremonial purposes. There is at least one in every pueblo. They are "off limits" to visitors.

What is the Indian Market?

An annual street market featuring the work of Indian artists and craftsmen. Entries are juried so the quality is high. Prizes are awarded for the best in each division. Indians from all over participate in the market. It is held on a weekend in August (dates vary from year to year) and the Chamber of Commerce will have the dates.

OUTDOORS

What birds will be seen around Santa Fe?

Bluebirds, roadrunners, ravens, hawks, jays, mockingbirds, towhees, grosbeak, robins, sparrows and wild canaries.

What kinds of fish are found in or near this area?

Various kinds of trout are found in these higher elevation streams.

What are some of the wild animals who live in the area?

Deer, bear, fox, coyotes and jackrabbits.

What are the names of some of the common shrubs and plants in the area?

Chamisa, sagebrush, yucca, pyracantha and saltbrush.

Is cactus native to this area?

Yes, not the giant cactus (saguaro) but smaller ones such as cholla, pricklypear, and barrel cactus.

What are the names of some of the trees in this area?

Pinon, juniper, Russian olive, cottonwood, poplar, willow, aspen, tamarisk, spruce and pine.

What are the mountains that surround Santa Fe?

The Sangre de Cristo (north and east), Sandias and Ortiz (south) and the Jemez (Hay-mess) mountains (west).

What is the nearest state part where I can hike or camp?

Hyde Memorial State Park (320 acres)

Where is it located?

Eight miles northeast of Santa Fe on the Hyde Park (Ski Basin) Road.

Where is the nearest national forest?

Santa Fe National Forest (1,526,489 acres)

How do I get there?

Since it covers such a wide area, there are many different sections. Consult a map or call the U.S. Forest Service for information. (They are listed in the telephone book.)

Where is the nearest wilderness area?

Pecos Wilderness (167,416 acres)

How do I get there?

Southeast on U.S. 84-85.

Is it easy to get lost in the wilderness area?

Yes. You can also get lost in any outdoor area. Stick to established paths and trails. Stay with your party. If you are going in alone, leave word at your motel or with someone about where you are going and when you expect to return. You might want to use a guidebook such as "6 1-Day Walks in the Pecos Wilderness of New Mexico" by Carl Overhage.

Where are the nearest Indian ruins?

Pecos State Monument, 27 miles southeast on U.S. 84-85. Pecos Pueblo was built in the 14th century. Here are also the ruins of the Franciscan Mission built in 1617.

Where is there another nearby group of Indian ruins?

At Bandelier National Monument (29,660 acres) where there are also camping and picnic sites, a museum, hiking trails and guided tours.

How do I get there?

It is 46 miles northwest of Santa Fe; take U.S. 285 to N.M. 4.

Where can I get fishing and hunting information?

At the New Mexico Dept. of Game and Fish located in the Villagra Building on Galisteo St.

Where can I picnic in downtown Santa Fe?

The Santa Fe River Park is on Alameda Street, two blocks south of the Plaza. It covers several blocks and has benches, picnic tables and at its west end (toward Guadalupe St.) a playground.

SPORTS

Are there any professional sports teams in Santa Fe?

No.

Is there a race track in or near Santa Fe?

Yes. Santa Fe Downs, ten miles south of the Plaza on U.S. 85.

Is there skiing in Santa Fe?

Yes, 16 miles northeast (Hyde Park Road) to the Santa Fe Ski Basin. There are chair lifts and a variety (29+) of trails.

How about cross-country skiing?

It is very popular and there are cross-country ski trails in Los Alamos and the Tesuque areas.

What other sports facilities are available in Santa Fe?

There are several municipal swimming pools and tennis courts. There are private tennis clubs which accept visitors for a fee. The Santa Fe Country Club golf course is also open to visitors for a fee. There are also bowling alleys.

MISCELLANEOUS

What is an old Spanish cemetery called?

A camposanto ("holy field")

Is there a National Cemetery in Santa Fe?

Yes, north on U.S. 285, 1½ miles from the Plaza.

What does "Anglo" mean?

Locally, it means any person not of Spanish descent.

What is a "primo"?

Primo means "cousin" (prima for women). It also implies a close, friendly relationship of mutual dependence and respect.

Who were Los Cinco Pintores?

Five young painters who came to Santa Fe in 1920 - Josef Bakos, Walter Mruk, Fremont Ellis, Willard Nash, and Will Shuster.

What are the strings of chile called?

Ristras (reece-strahs). They are hung outside to aid in the drying process and are hung on portals for their decorative effect. They are hung inside, particularly in kitchens where they are both decorative and useful.

Are there any dude ranches here?

Bishop's Lodge (Bishop's Lodge Rd.)
Rancho Encantado (Tesuque)

RECOMMENDED READING

Adobe Architecture *(Myrtle Stedman)*
Artists of the Canyons & Caminos, The Early Years *(Edna Robertson and Sarah Nestor)*
Centuries of Santa Fe *(Paul Horgan)*
Christmas in Old Santa Fe *(Pedro R. Ortega)*
City Different and the Palace, The *(Rosemary Nusbaum)*
Death Comes for the Archbishop *(Willa Cather)*
Delight Makers *(Adolph Bandelier)*
Eagle in the Sky *(Frank McCulloch)*
First Ladies of New Mexico, The *(Eunice Kalloch and Ruth K. Hall)*
Good Life: New Mexico Traditions and Food, The *(Fabiola C. de Baca Gilbert)*
Great Kiva, The *(Phillips Kloss)*
House At Otowi Bridge, The *(Peggy Pond Church)*

House Made of Dawn *(N. Scott Momaday)*
Lamy of Santa Fe *(Paul Horgan)*
Light & Color: Images from New Mexico *(Museum of Fine Arts, Santa Fe, NM)*
Living Legends *(Alice Bullock)*
Loretto and the Miraculous Staircase *(Alice Bullock)*
Man With the Calabash Pipe *(Oliver LaFarge)*
Maria Making Pottery *(Hazel Hyde)*
Maria, the Legend, the Legacy *(Susan B. McGreevy)*
Maria, the Potter of San Ildefonso *(Alice Marriott)*
Masked Gods, Navaho and Pueblo Ceremonials *(Frank Waters)*
Mexican Cookbook, The *(Erna Fergusson)*
Milagro Beanfield War *(John Nichols)*
Mother Ditch, The *(Oliver LaFarge)*
Mountain Villages *(Alice Bullock)*
New Mexico Place Names *(Thomas M. Pearce)*
No High Adobe *(Dorothy L. Pillsbury)*
Old Santa Fe Today *(Historic Santa Fe Foundation)*
Pueblo Indian Cookbook *(Phyllis Hughes)*
Red Sky At Morning *(Richard Bradford)*
Santa Fe and Taos, the Writer's Era, 1916-1941 *(Marta Weigle and Kyle Fiore)*
Santa Fe, the City Different *(Justine Thomas)*
Santos and Saints' Days *(Drew Bacigalupa)*
Summer People/Winter People, A Guide to Pueblos in the Santa Fe Area *(Sandra A. Edelman)*
Turquoise Mask (Phyllis A. Whitney)
Wind Leaves No Shadow, The *(Ruth L. Alexander)*

Most of these books are in print and can be purchased at bookstores, hotel/motel newsstands and gift shops and in many other area shops. Out-of-print books can be found at the public library and also sometimes at bookstores that carry old books.

These magazines are also recommended:

New Mexico Magazine
Santa Fean
New Mexico Wildlife

SOME SANTA FE BOOKSTORES

Ancient City Book Shop *(109 E. Palace Ave.)*
Books West *(Coronado Shopping Center)*
Collected Works *(208-B W. San Francisco)*
B. Dalton's *(DeVargas Mall)*
First Edition Book Store *(Lincoln Centre)*
La Fonda Newsstand *(La Fonda Hotel)*
Los Llanos Bookstore *(72 E. San Francisco)*
Museum of New Mexico Shops
Potter, Nicholas *(203 E. Palace Ave.)*
Santa Fe Bookseller *(203 W. San Francisco)*
Villagra Book Shop *(Sena Plaza)*

NOTES

NOTES

NOTES

NOTES

NOTES

NOTES